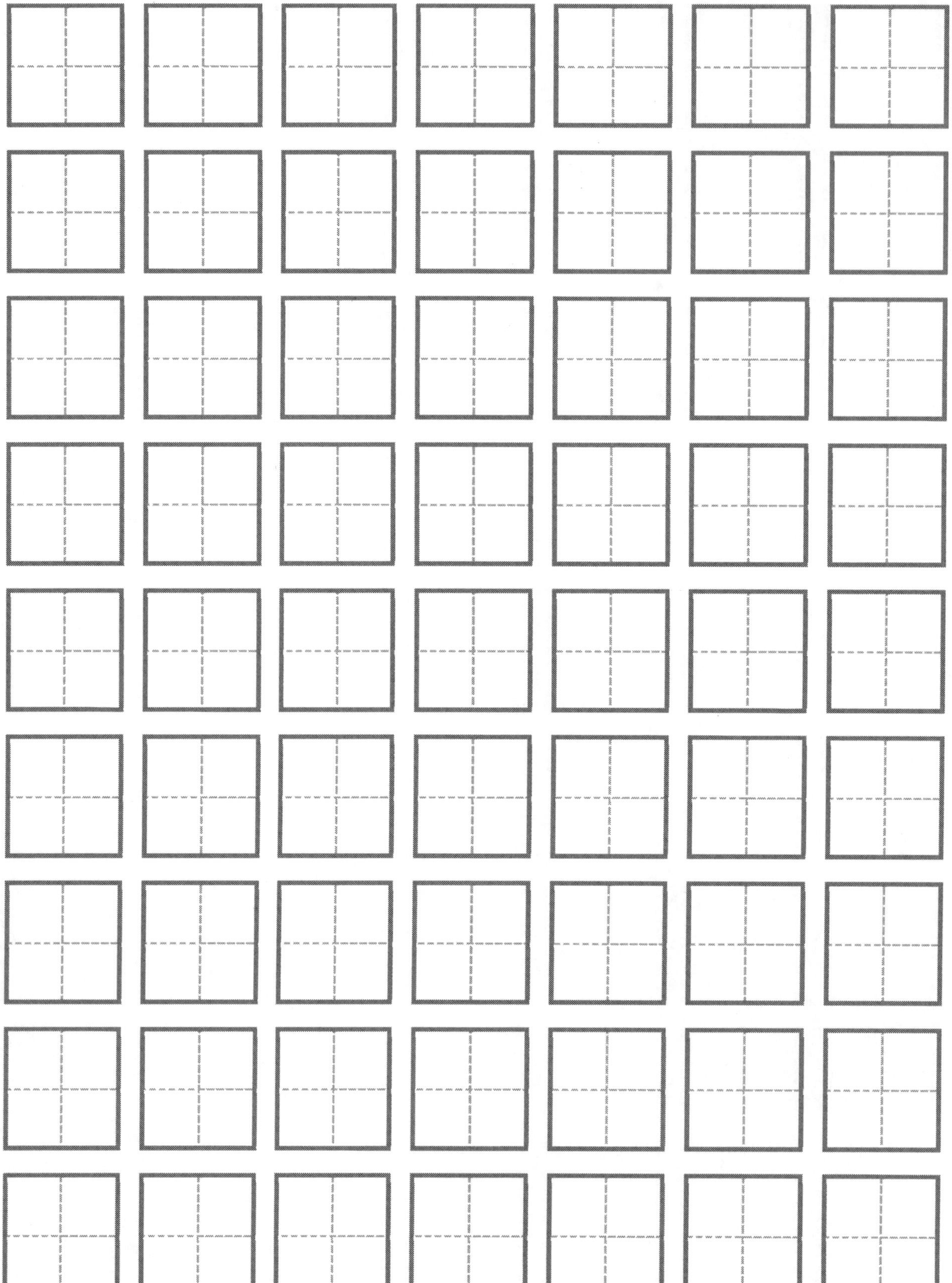

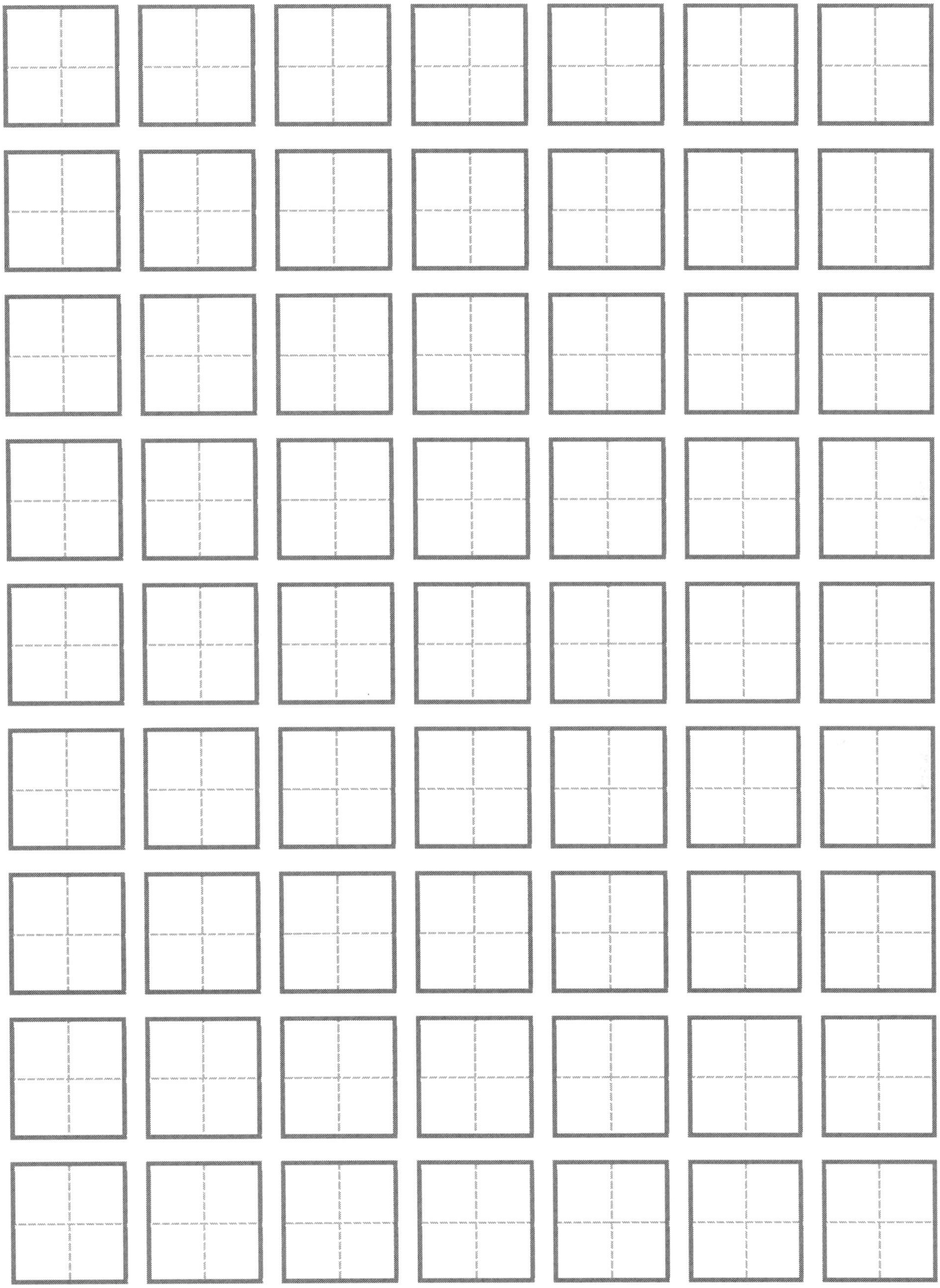

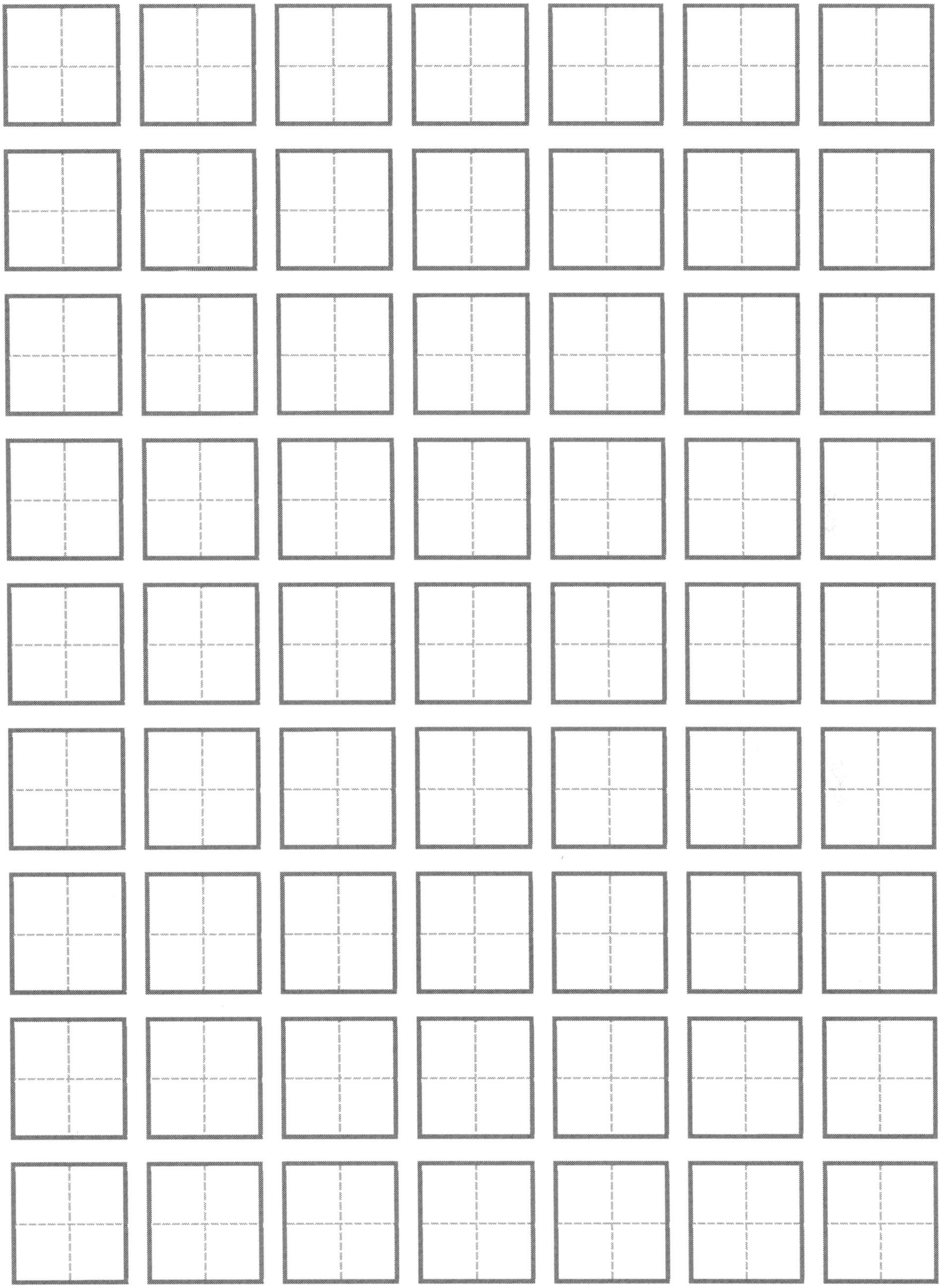

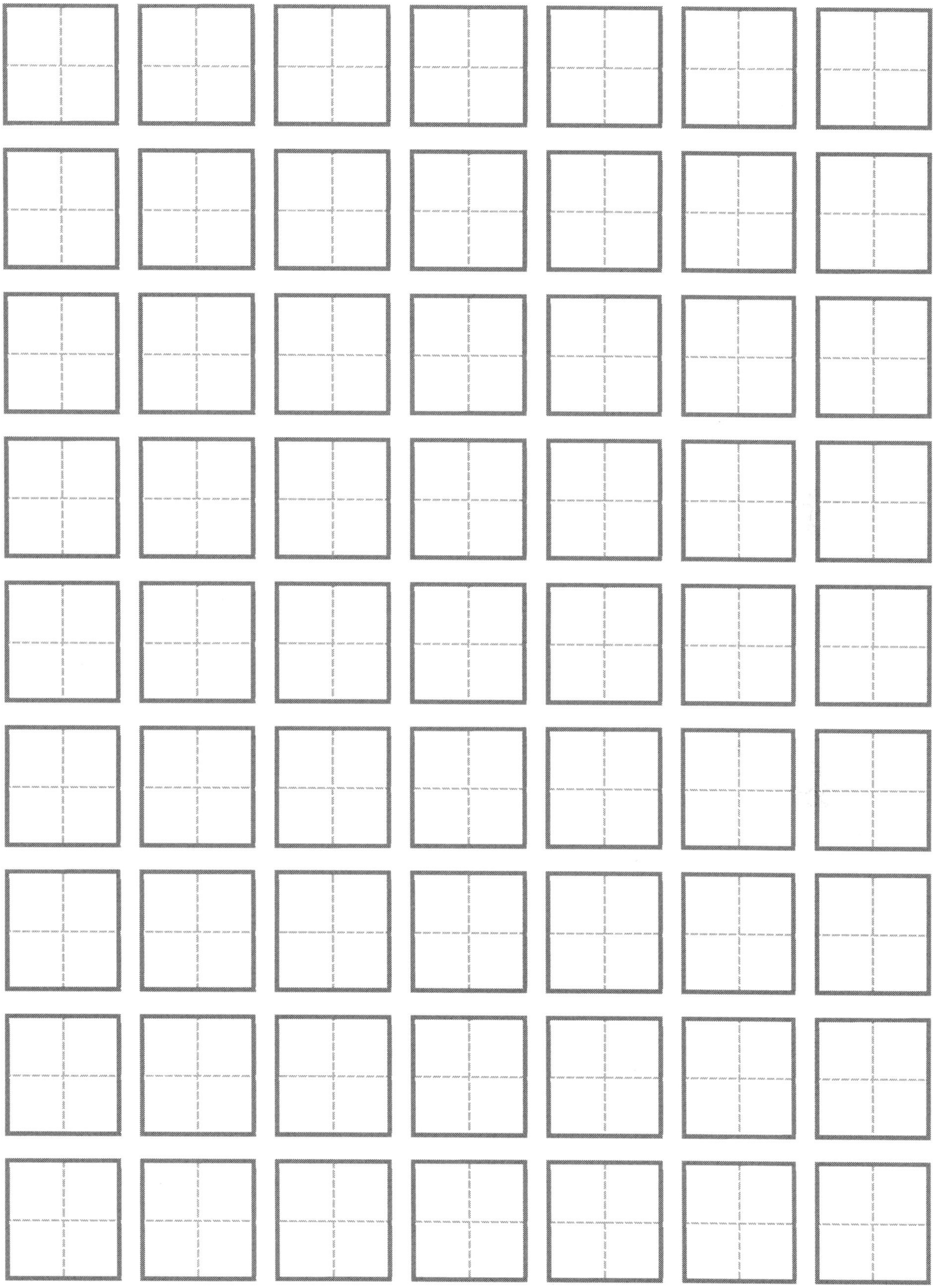

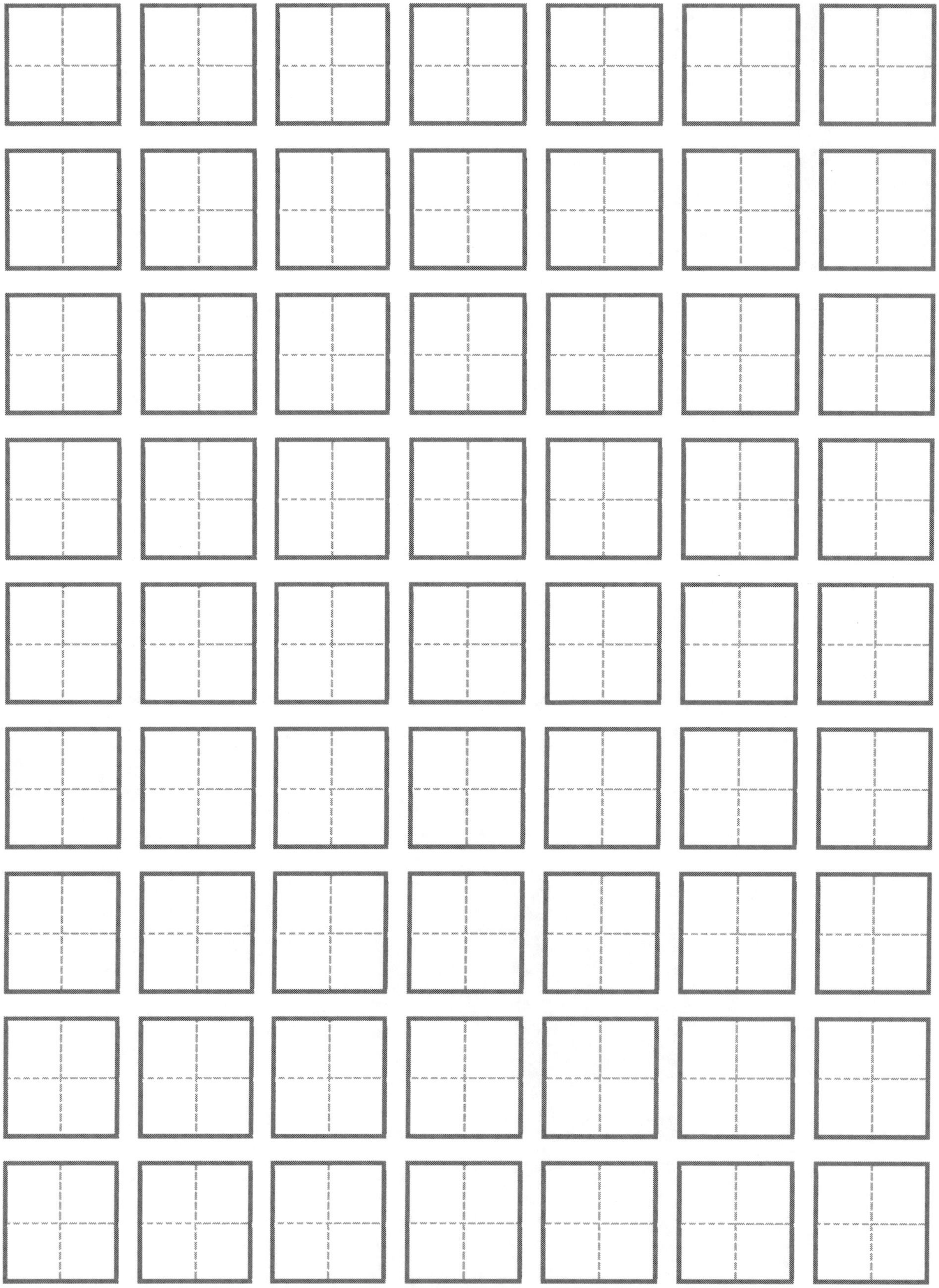

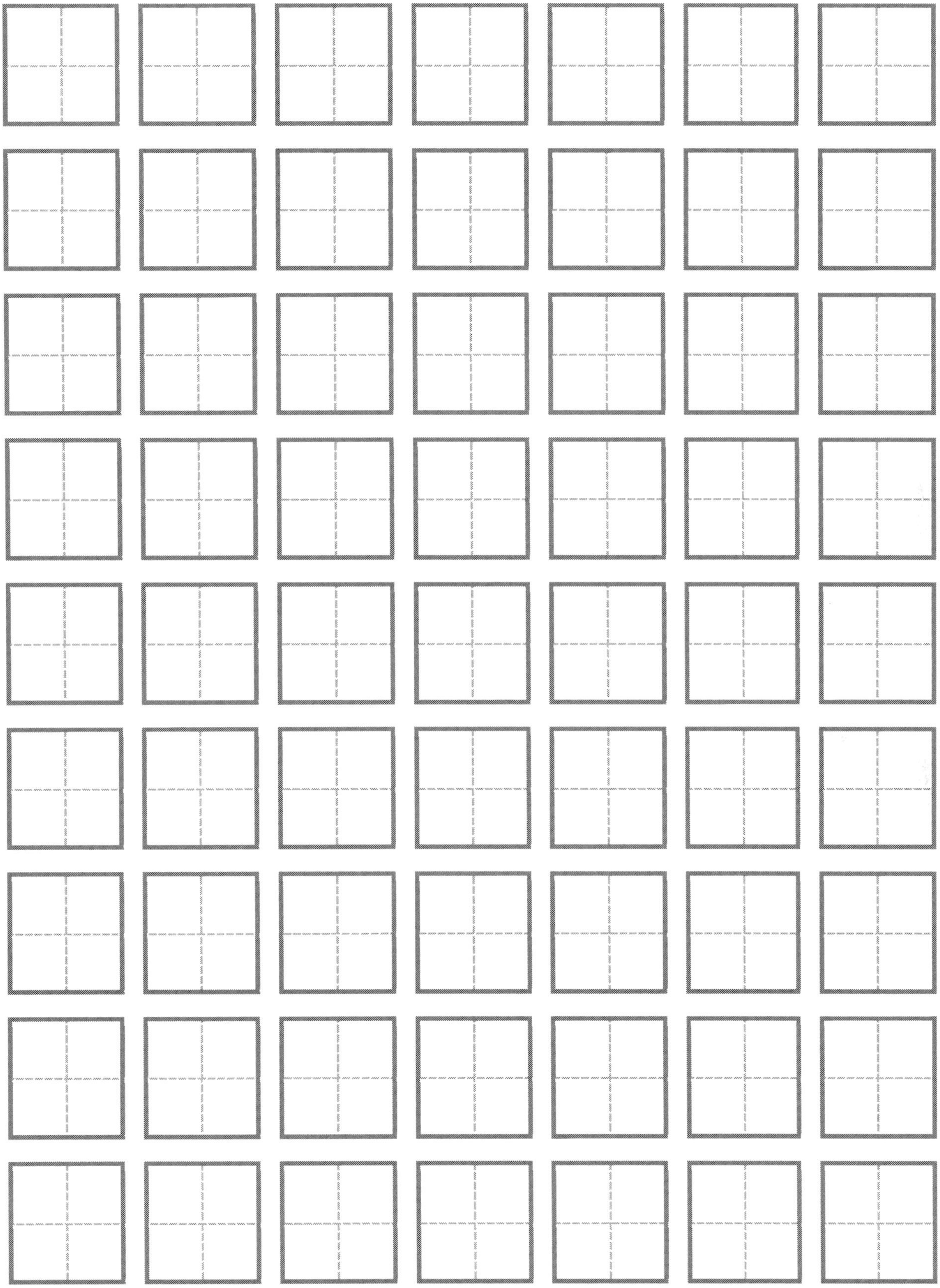

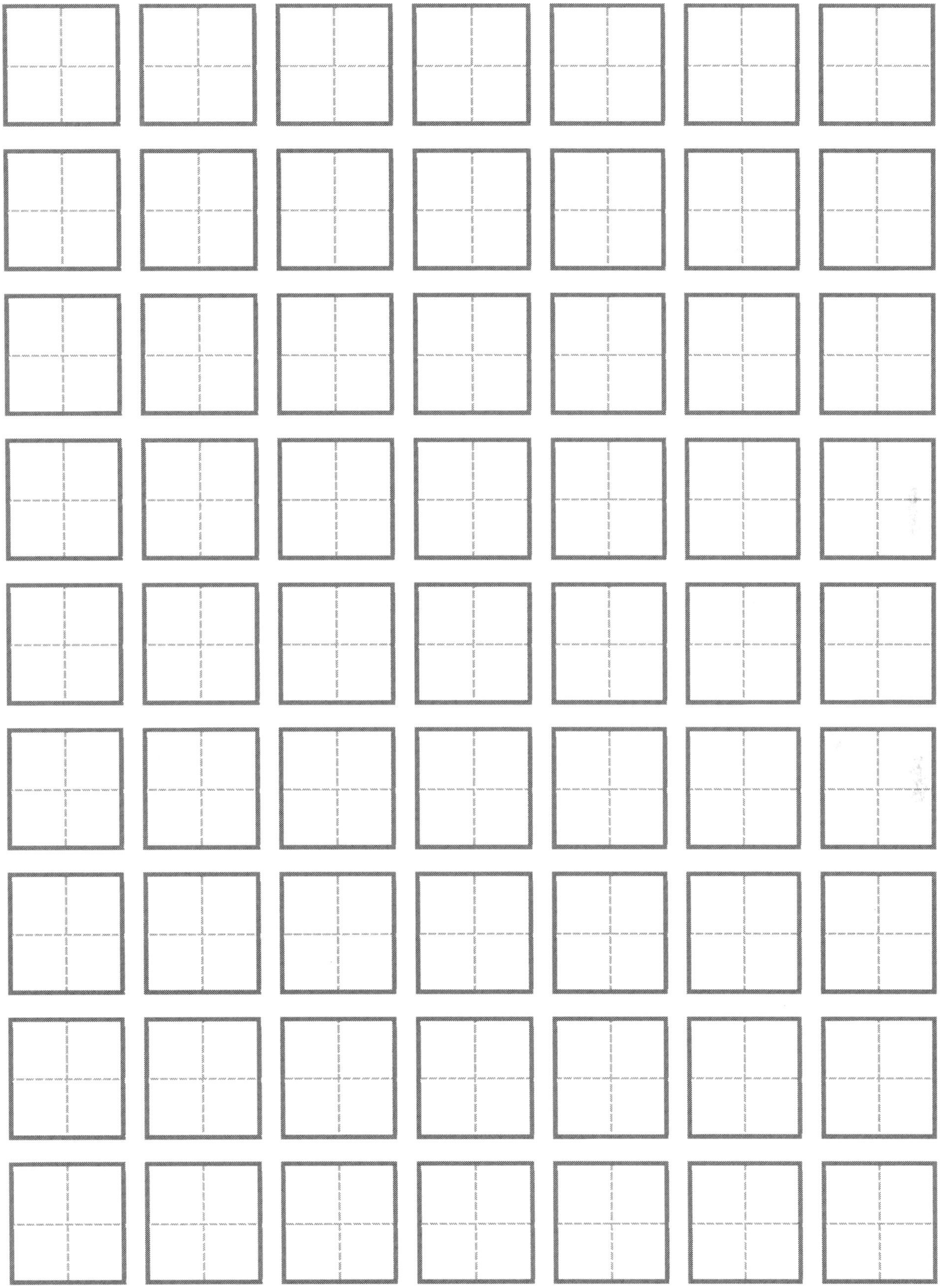

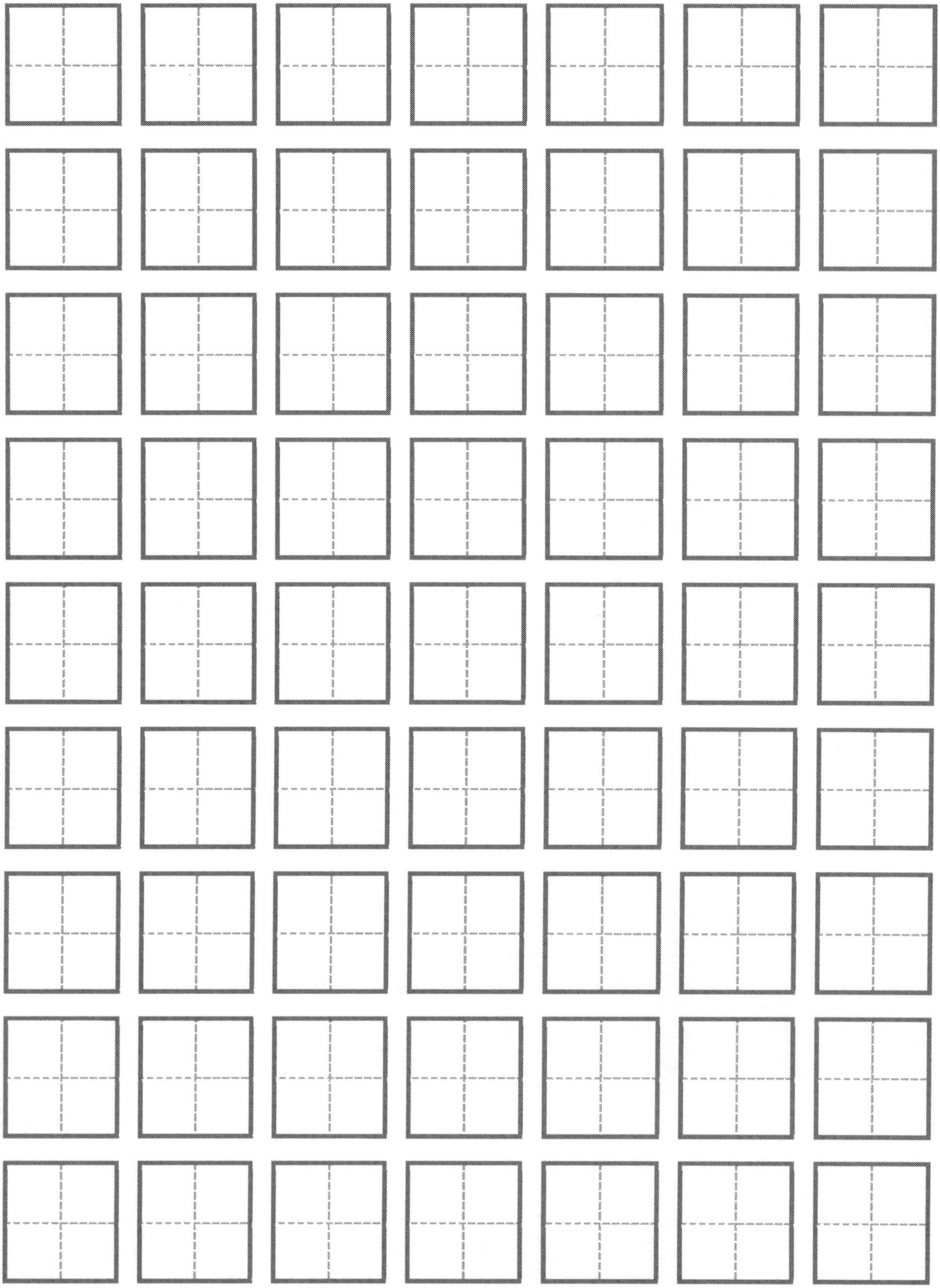

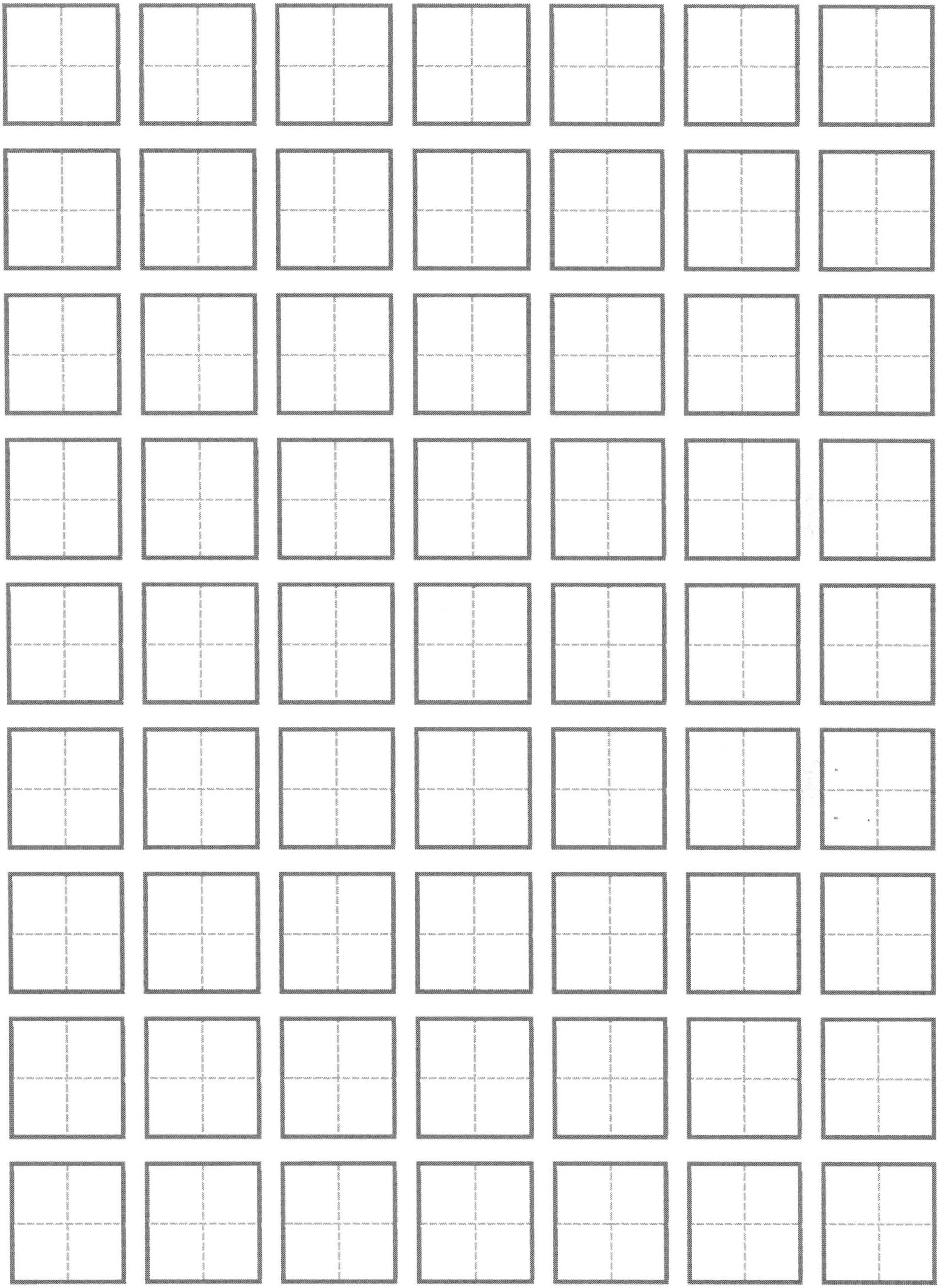

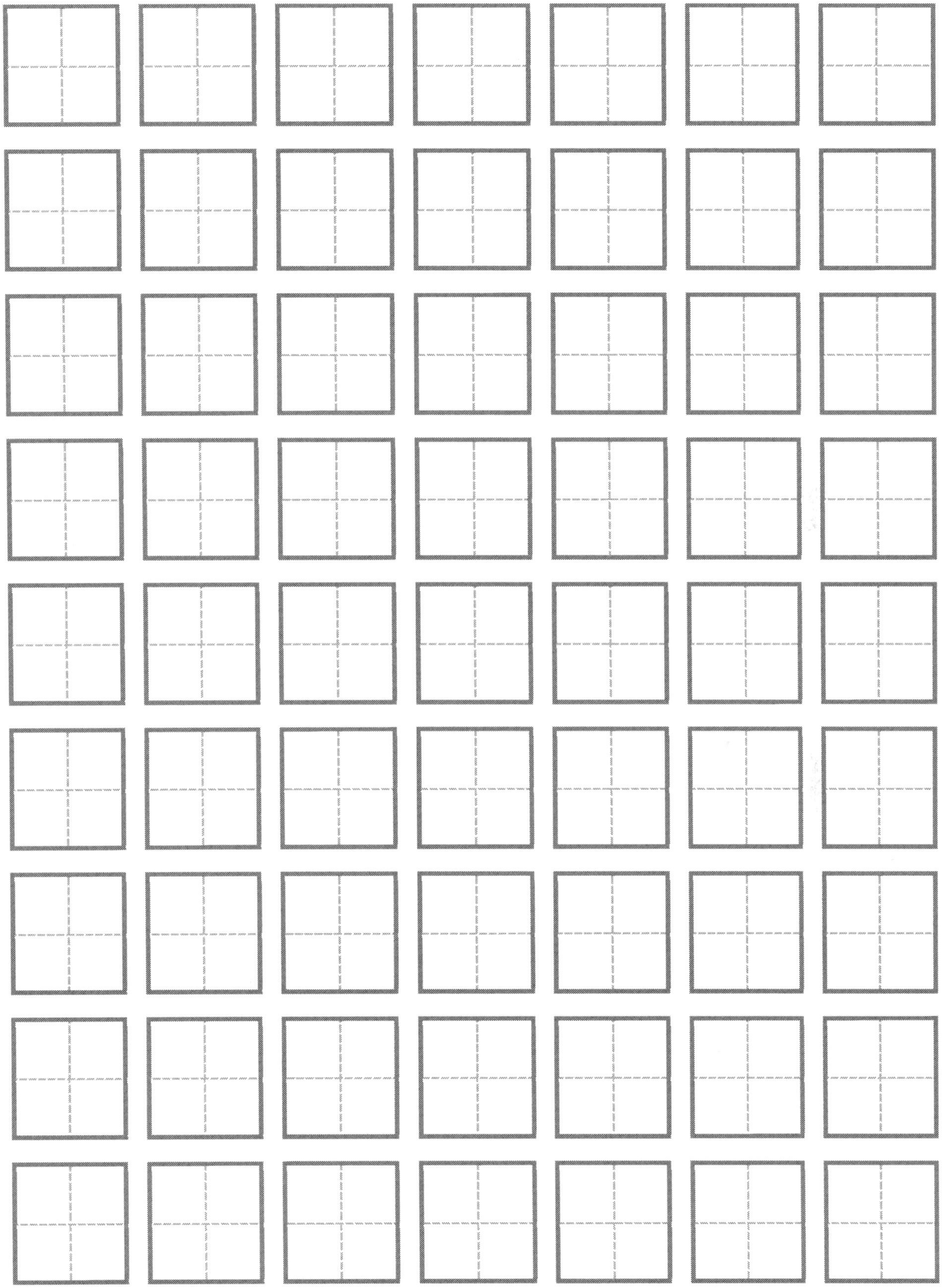

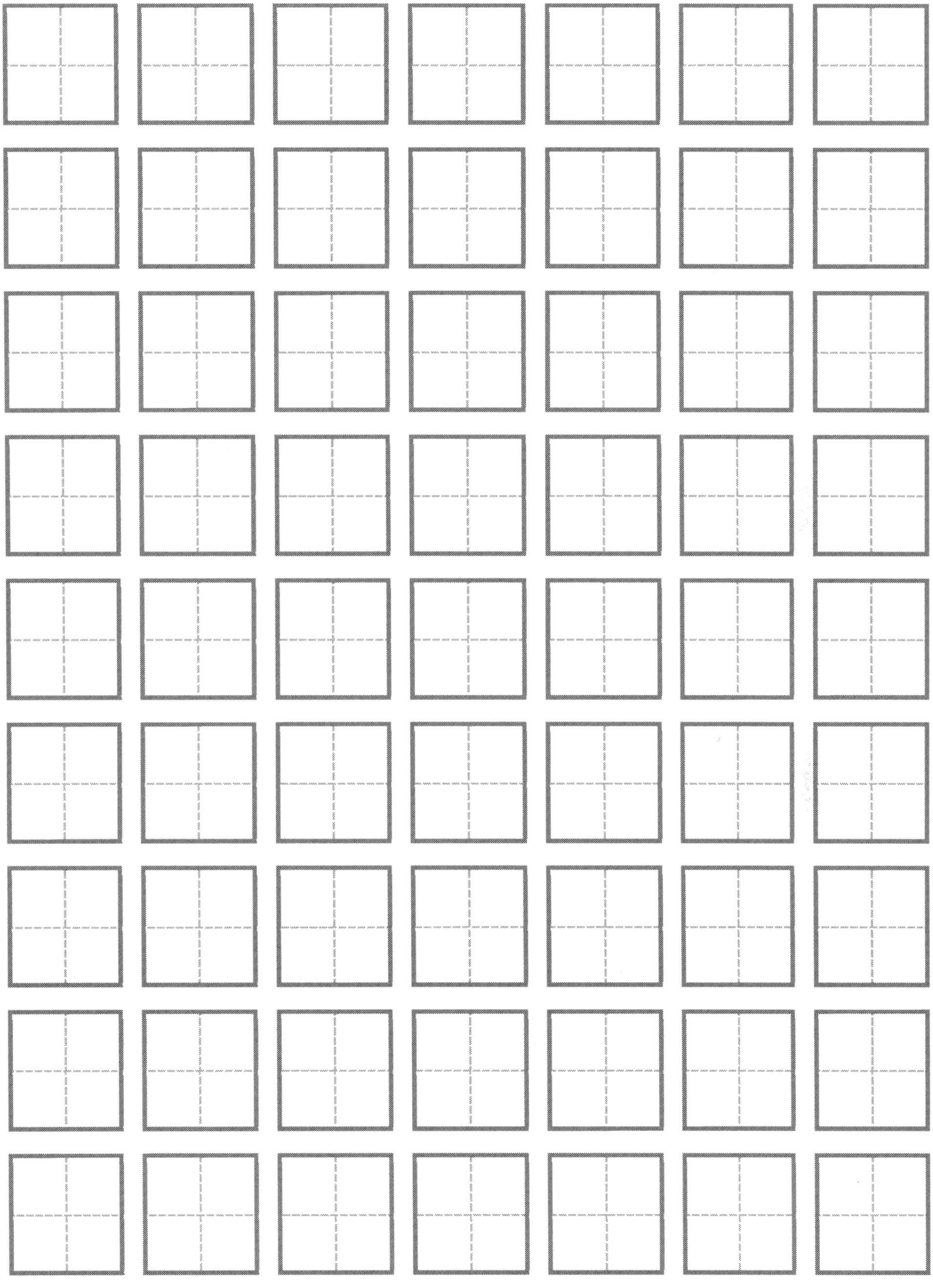

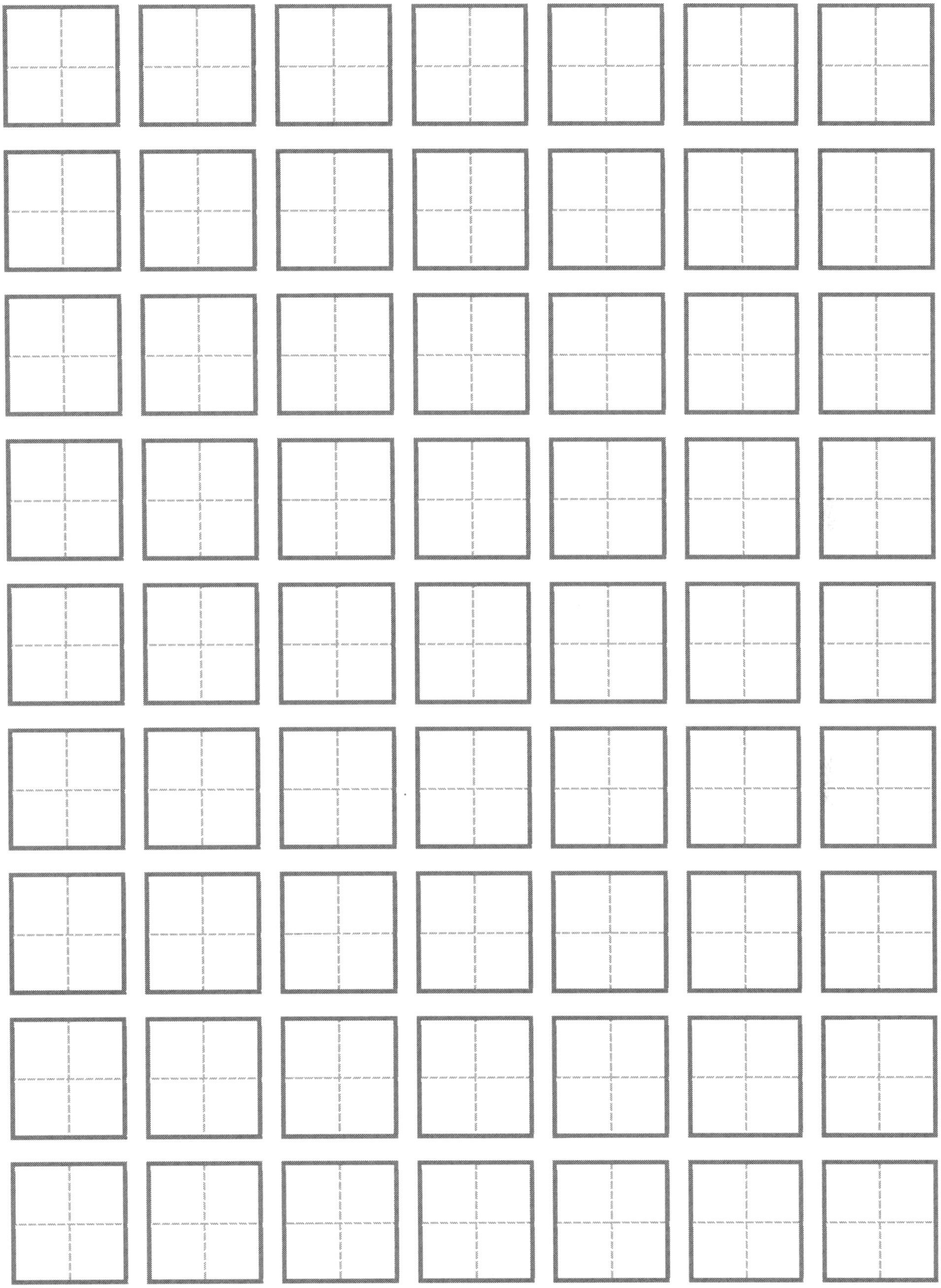

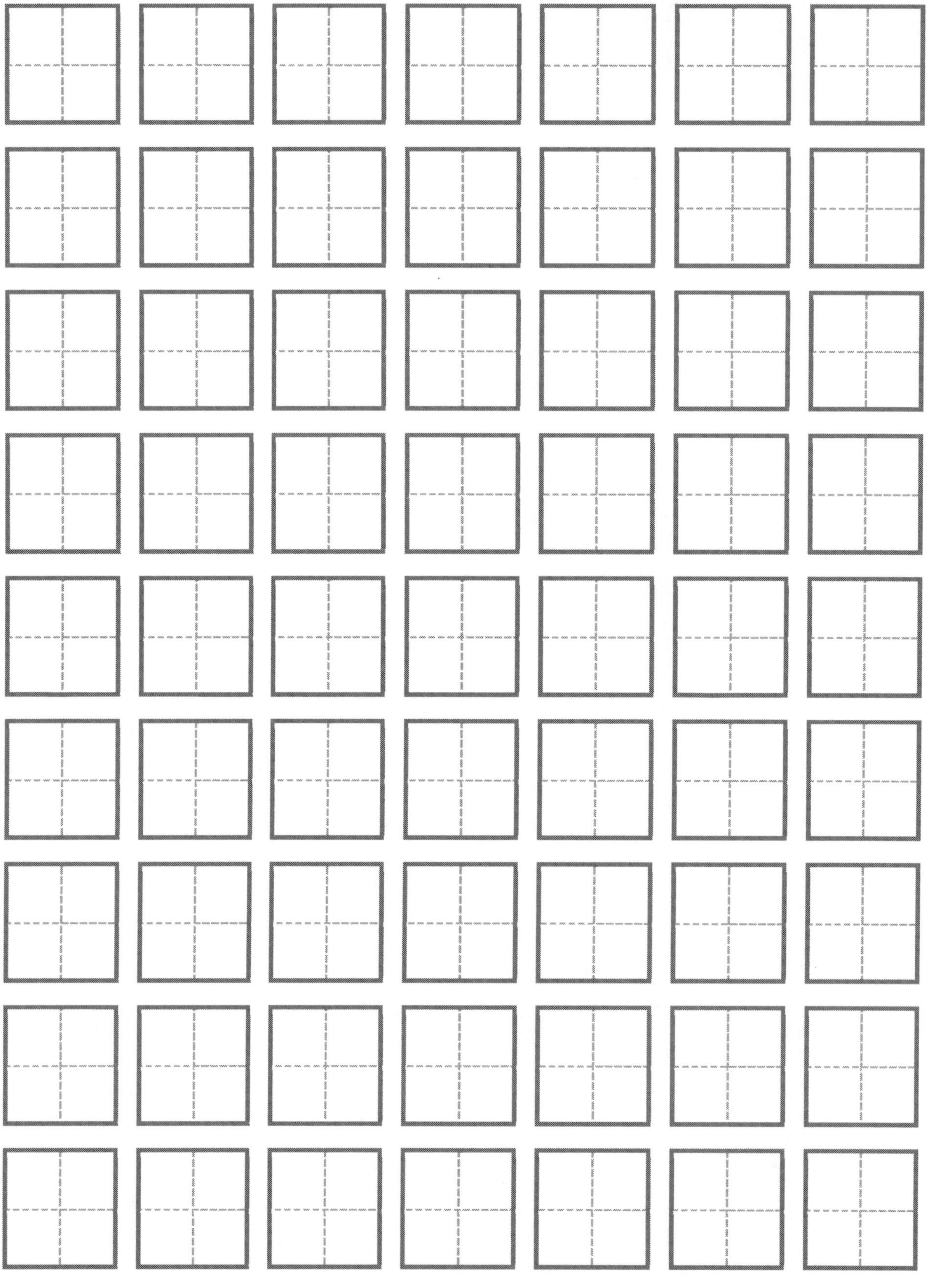

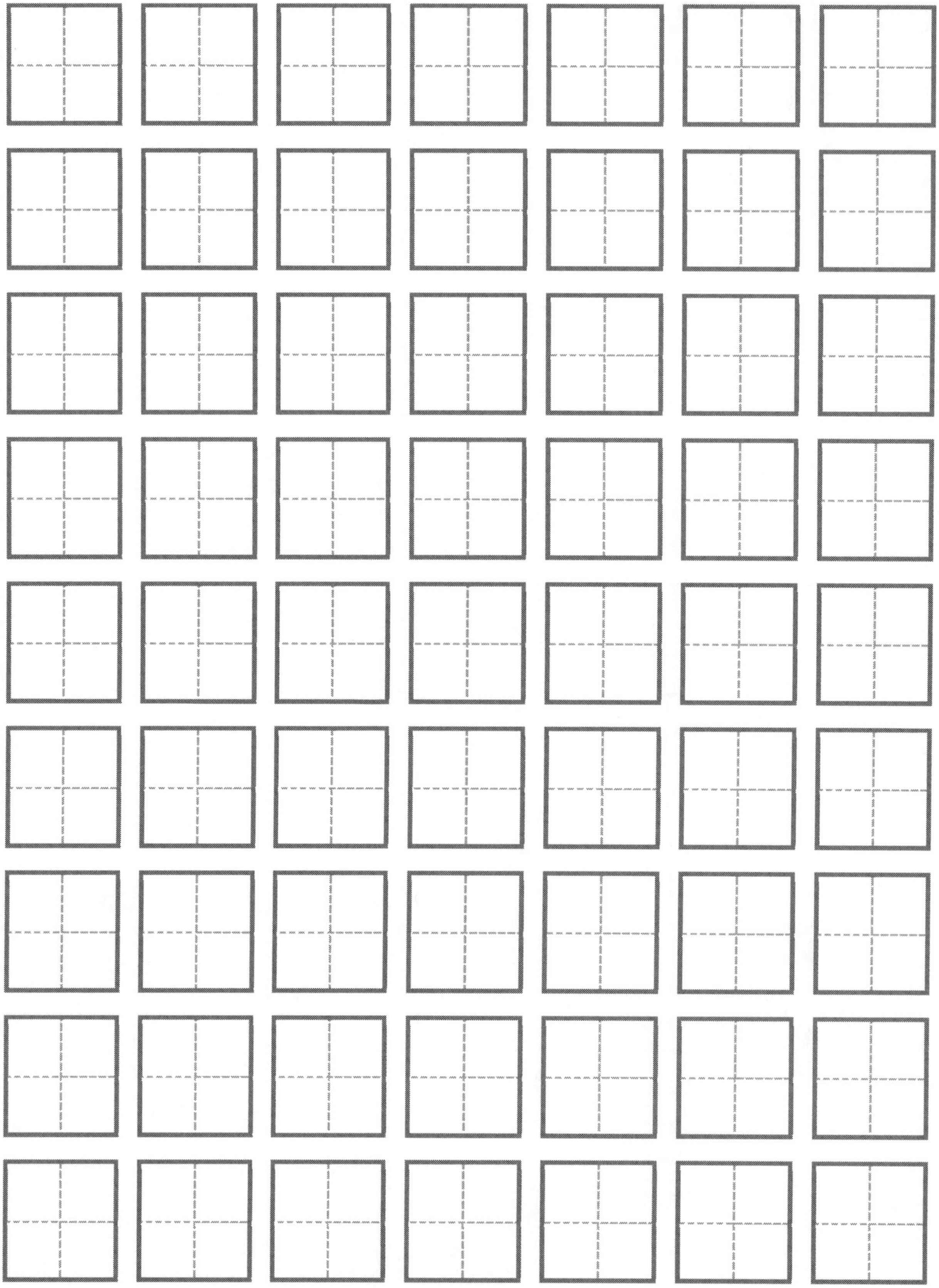

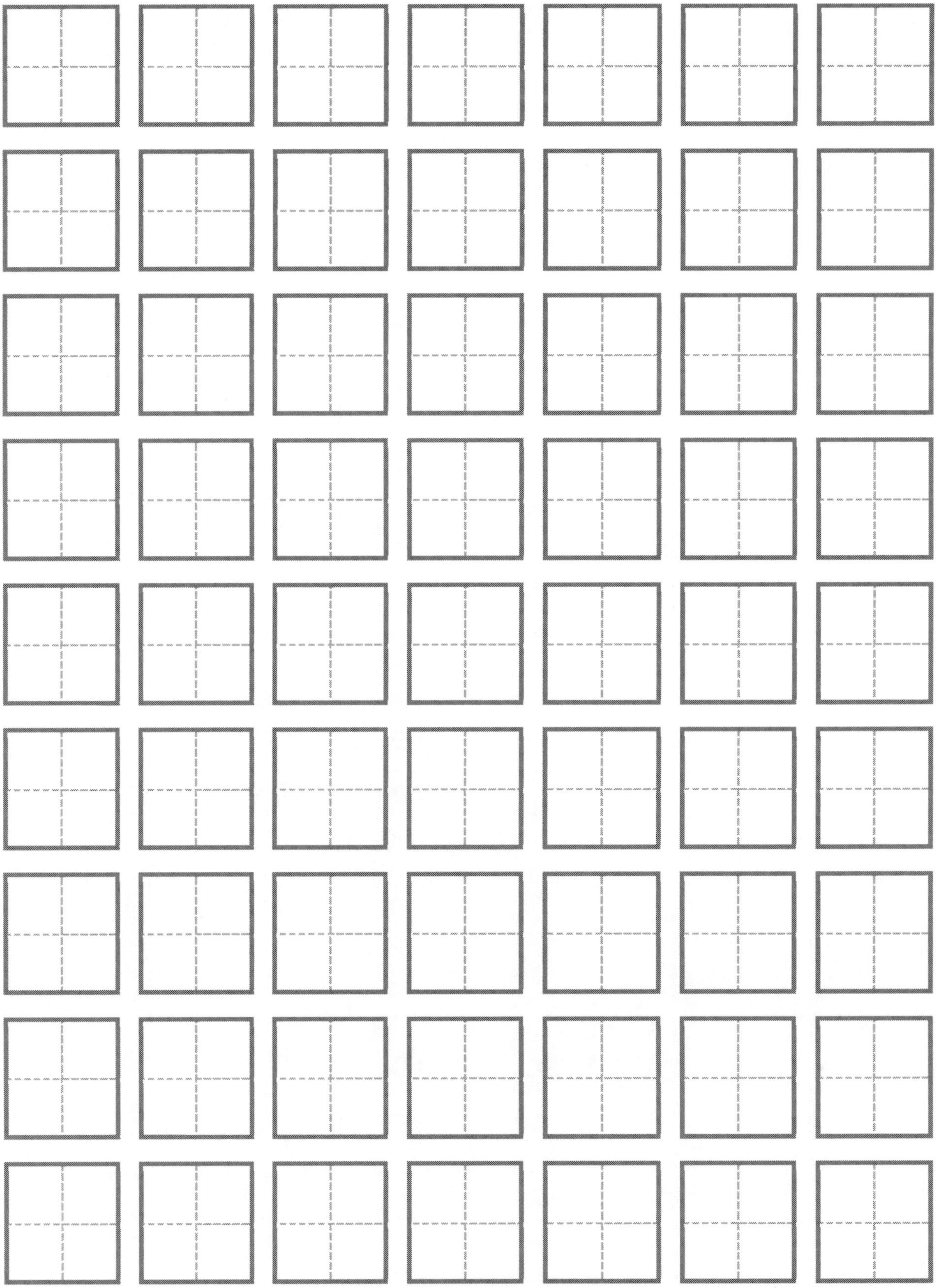

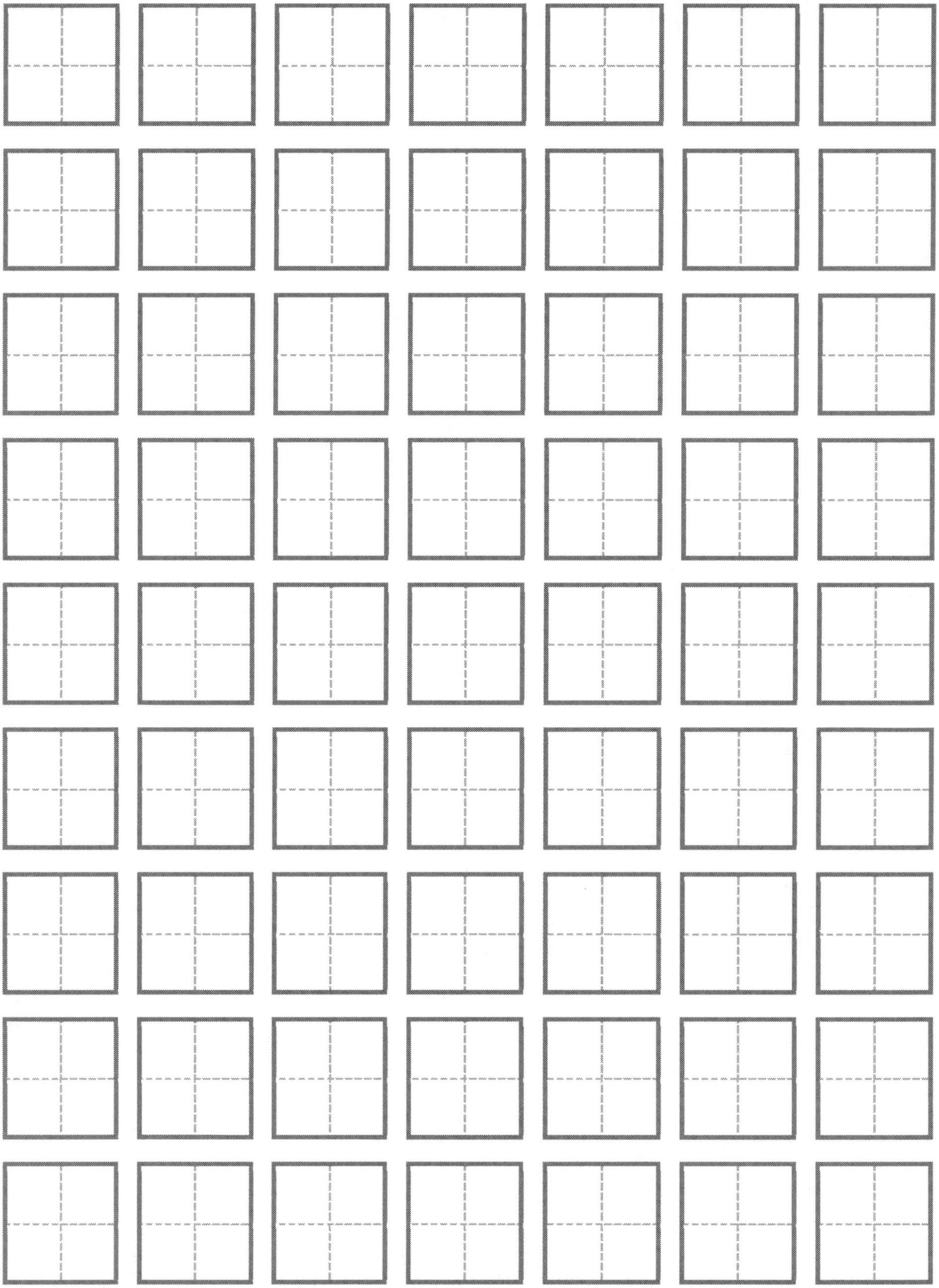

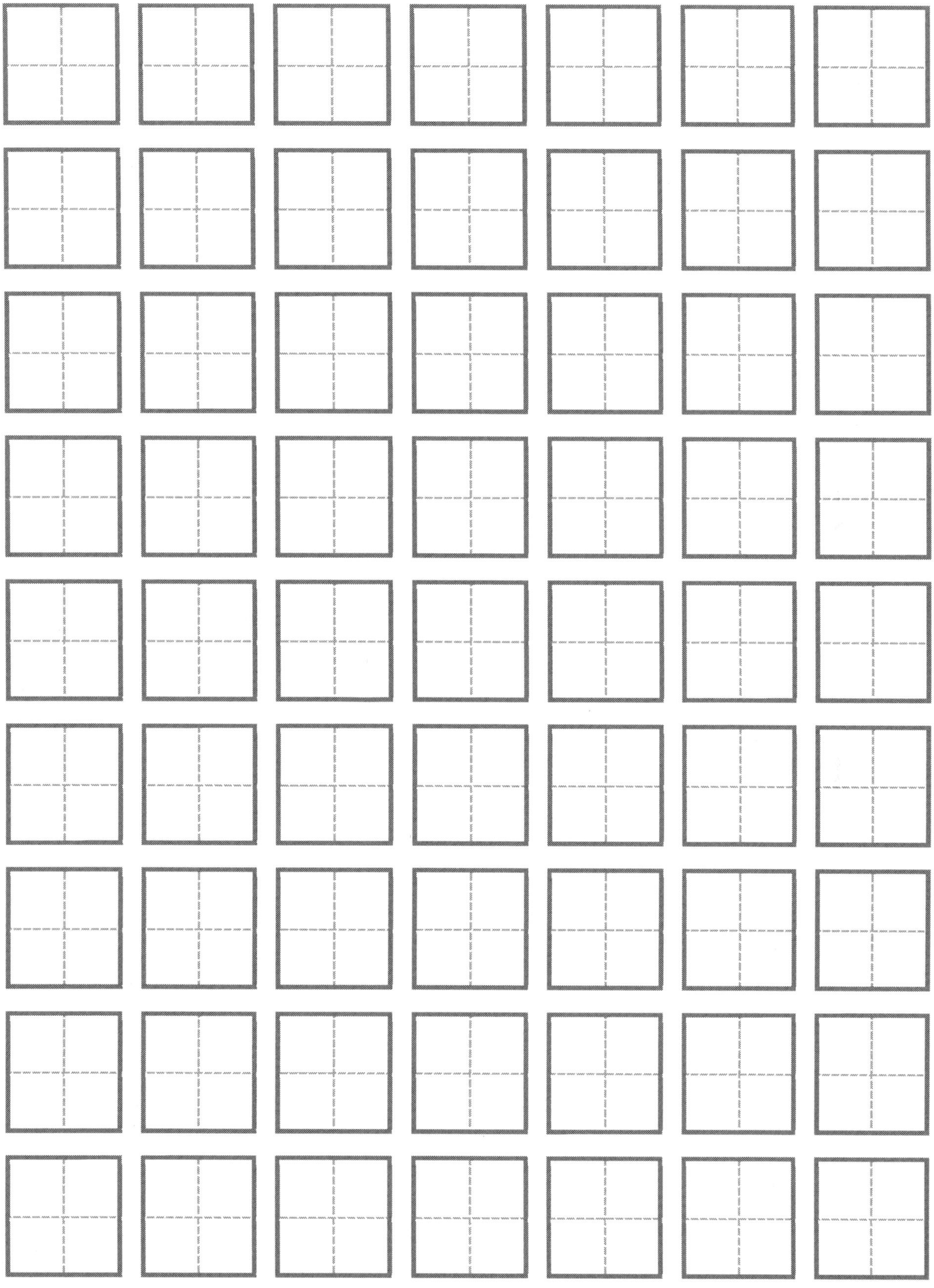

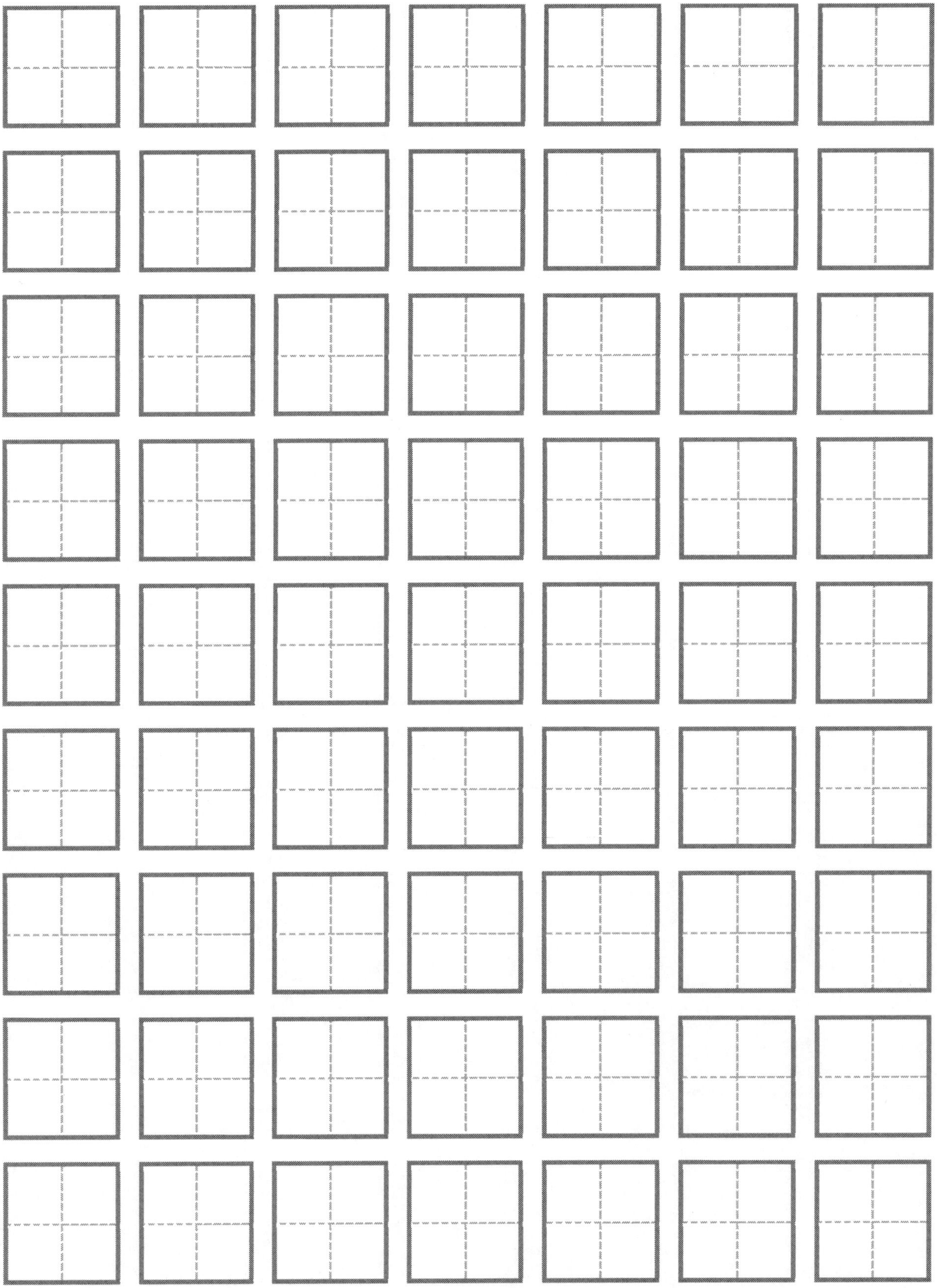

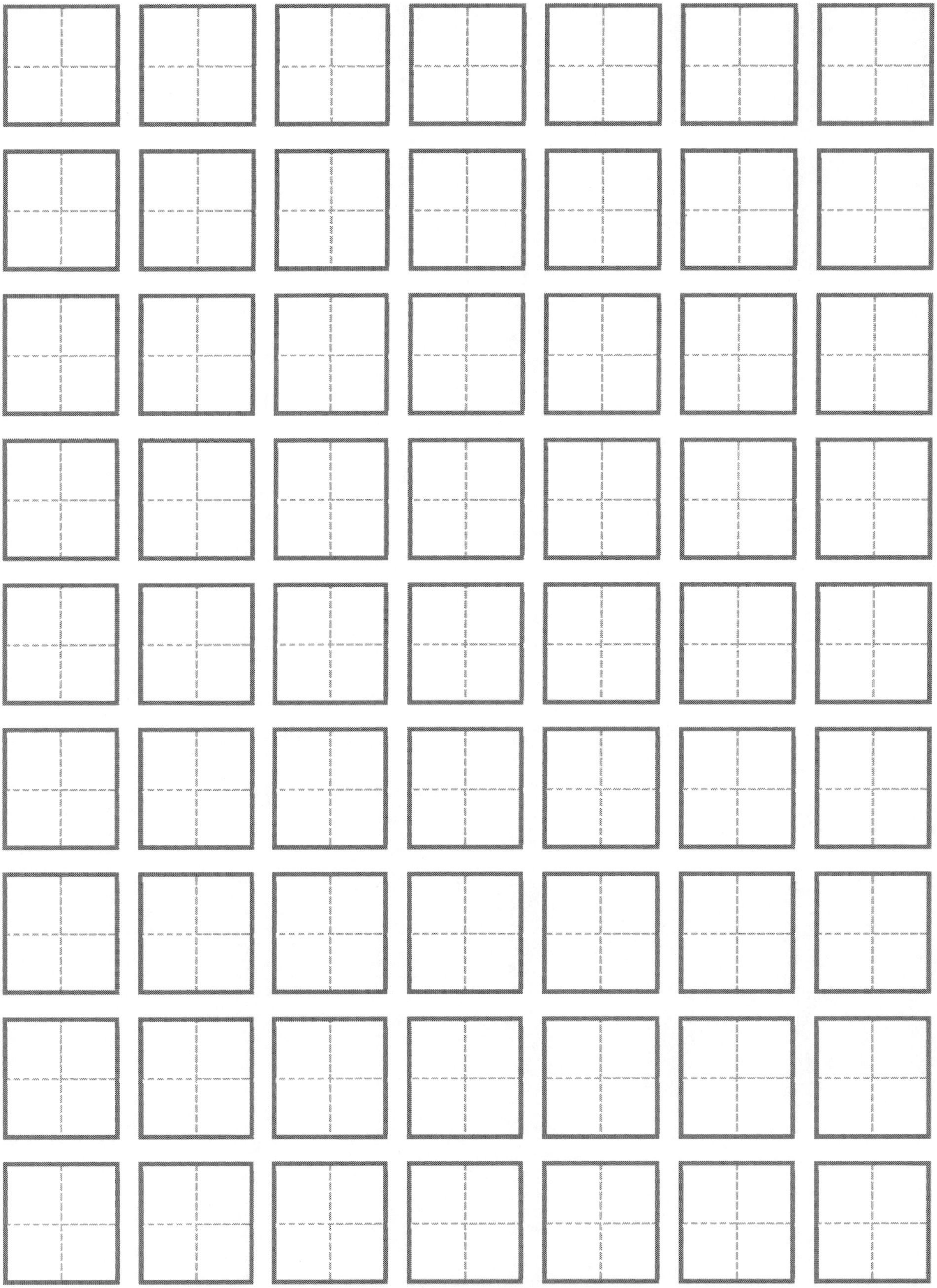

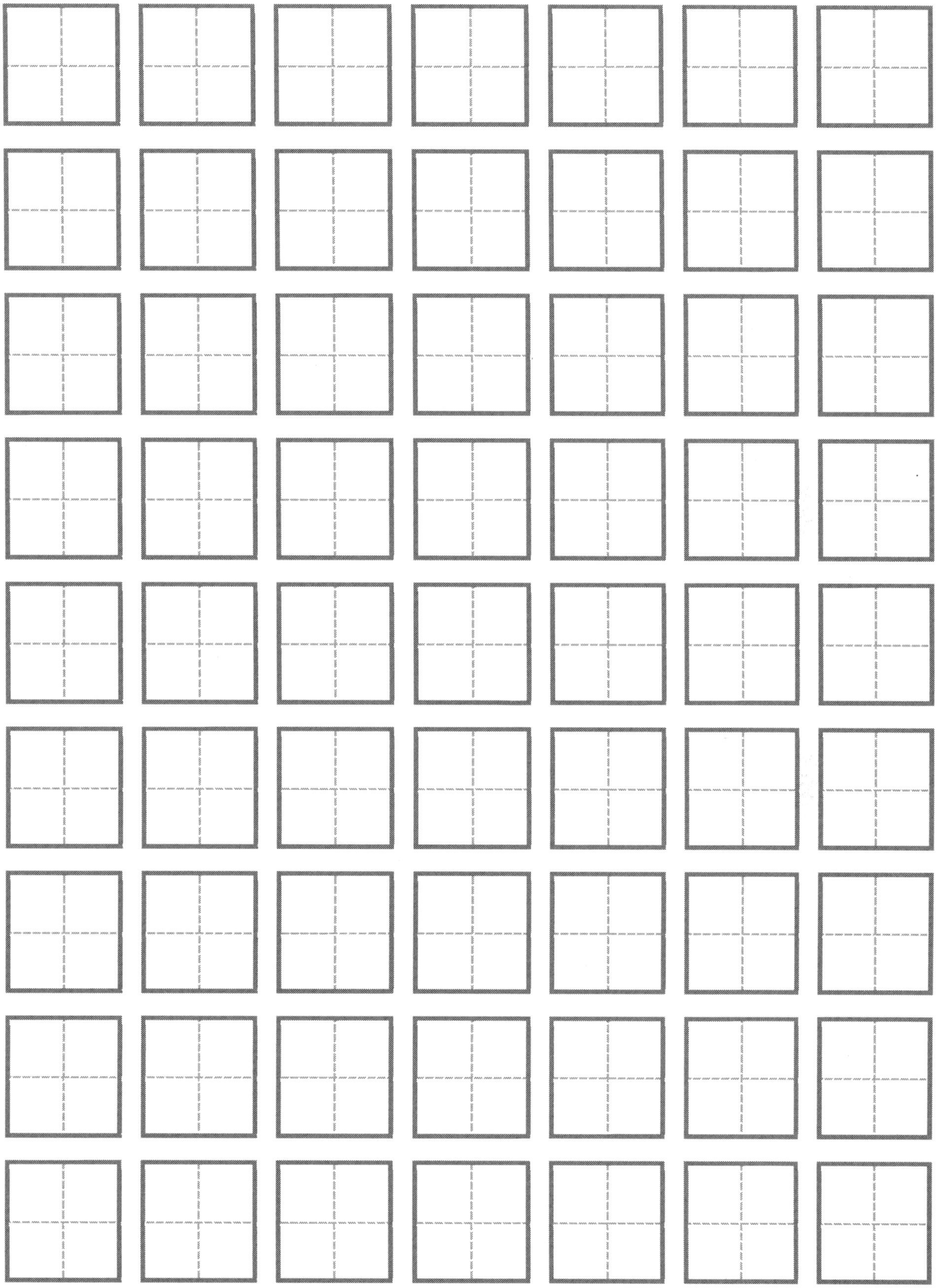

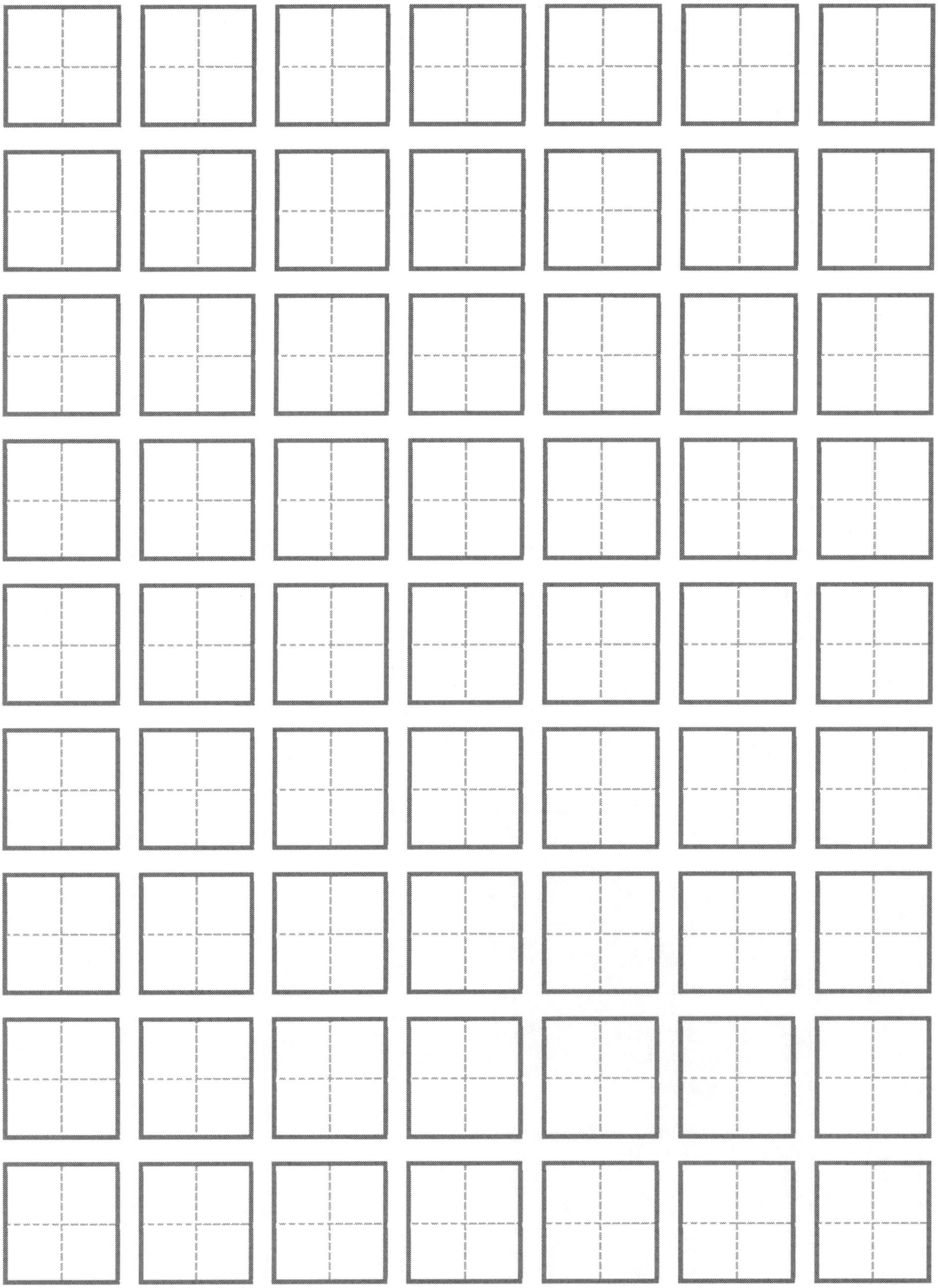

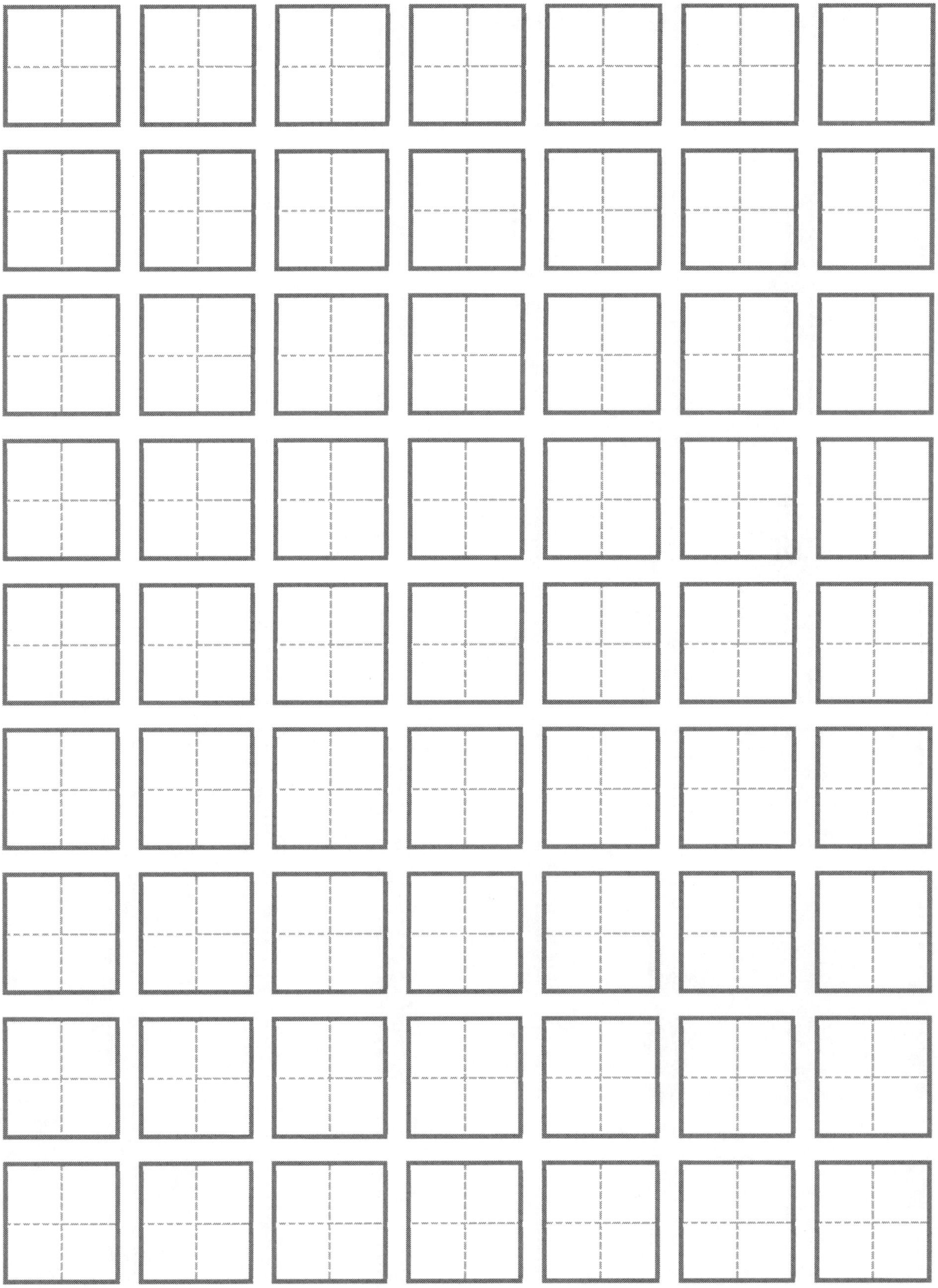

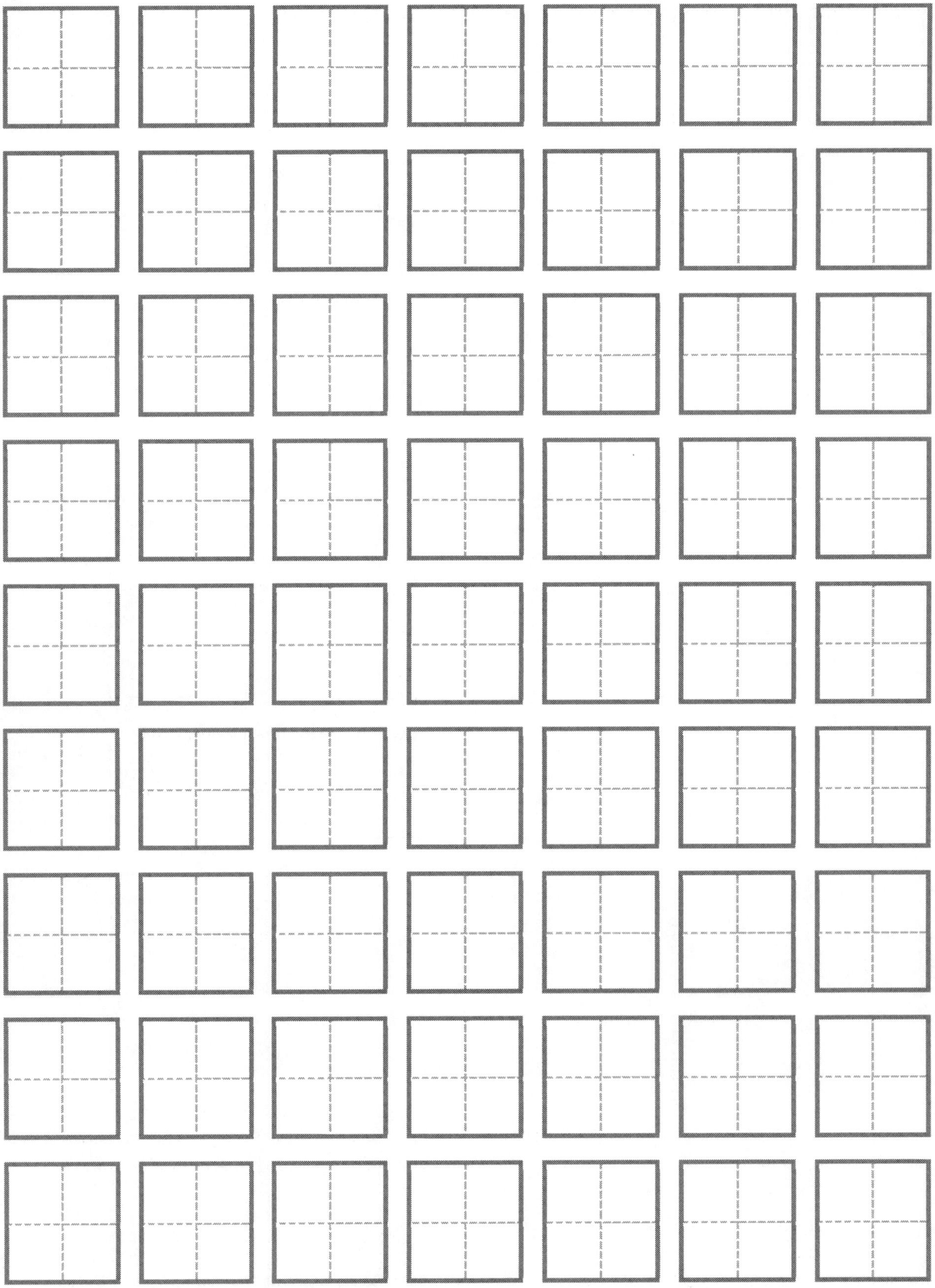

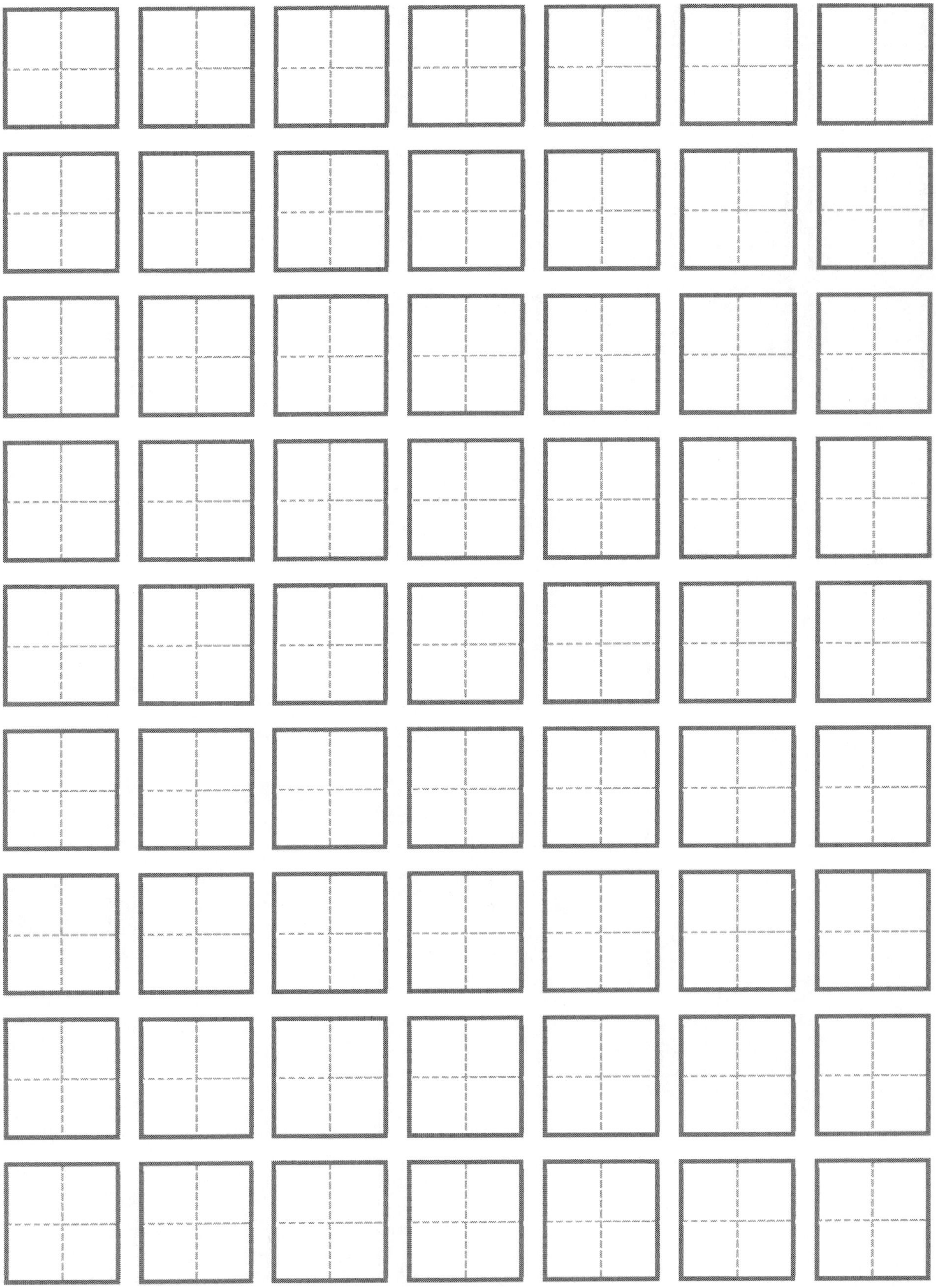

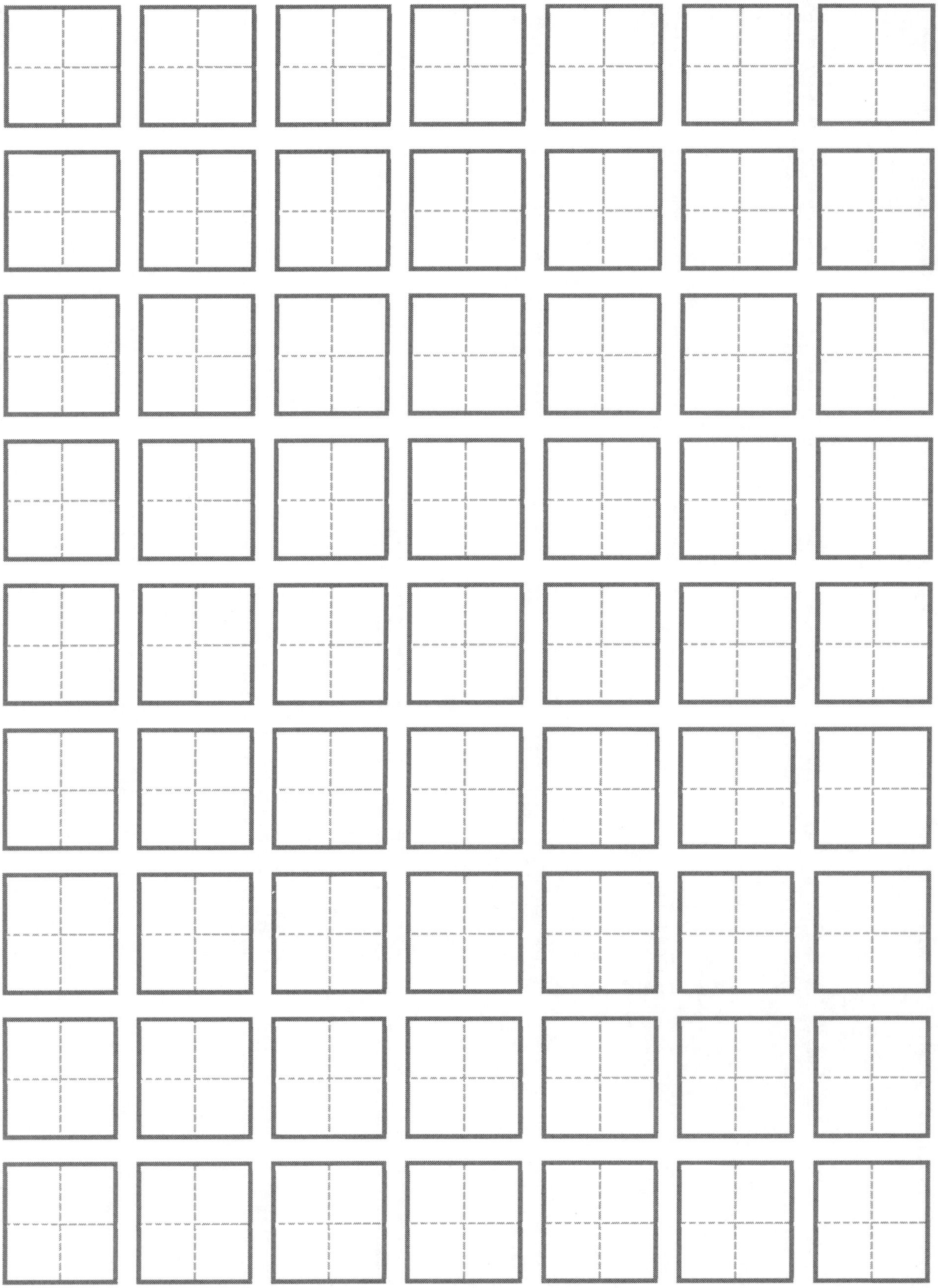

Made in the USA
Las Vegas, NV
09 January 2024

84087535R00061